PIANO * VOCAL * GUITAR

MALT SHOP Memories

ISBN 978-1-4234-5301-7

HAL•LEONARD®
CORPORATION
7777 W. BLUEMOUND RD. P.O. BOX 13819 MILWAUKEE, WI 53213

Visit Hal Leonard Online at
www.halleonard.com

ALL I HAVE TO DO IS DREAM

Words and Music by
BOUDLEAUX BRYANT

1
2
E♭ Cm A♭ B♭ E♭ A♭
3fr 3fr 4fr 3fr 4fr
dream, dream, dream, dream. When dream.
E♭ E♭7 A♭ Gm
I can make you mine, taste your lips of wine,
Fm B♭ E♭ E♭7 A♭
an - y - time, night or day. On - ly trou - ble is,
Gm F7 Fm7/B♭ B♭
gee whiz, I'm dream - ing my life a - way! I
3

E♭ Cm A♭ B♭ E♭ Cm
need you so, that I could die; I love you so,
A♭ B♭ E♭ Cm A♭ B♭
and that is why, when - ev - er I want you all I have to do is
1 E♭ A♭ E♭ E♭7
dream.
2 E♭ Cm
dream,
A♭ B♭ E♭ Cm A♭ B♭ E♭
dream, dream, dream, dream, dream, dream, dream, dream.
rit.

BABY LOVE

Words and Music by BRIAN HOLLAND,
EDWARD HOLLAND and LAMONT DOZIER

B♭6
F
B♭
Am
Wan-na know what did I do wrong to make you stay a -
Why you do me like you do, I guess it's me,
So deep in love with you. Ba - by, ba - by,
To Coda
Gm7
C7
F
F7
way so long. 'Cause, ba - by love, my ba - by love, been
ooh. Need to hold you once a - gain, my love, feel your
ooh. 'Til it
D7
Gm
3fr
B♭6
miss - ing ya, miss kiss - ing ya. In - stead of
warm em - brace, my love. Don't throw our
F
B♭6
break - ing up, let's start some kiss - ing and
love a - way, please don't do

F
B♭6
F
mak - ing up.
me this way.
Don't throw our love a - way,
Not hap - py like I used to be,
B♭
Am
1
Gm7
C9
2
Gm7
C9
D.C. al Coda
in my arms why don't you stay?
lone - li - ness has got the best of
CODA
F
F7
D7
hurt me, 'til it hurt me.
Ooh,
Gm
3fr
B♭6
F
Repeat and Fade
ba - by love, don't throw our love a - way.
Don't throw our love a - way.

ANGEL BABY

Words and Music by
ROSE HAMLIN

Dm7 G7 C Am Dm7 G7
my heart skips a beat, I can hard - ly stand on my own two feet,
C Am Dm7 G C Am
be - cause I love you, I love you I do, an - gel ba - by,
Dm7 G7 C Am Dm7 G7
my an - gel ba - by. Ooh, I love you, ooh, I do,
C Am Dm7 G7 C Am
no one could love you like I do. Ooh

Dm7 G7 C Am Dm7 G7
ooh ooh ooh.
C Am Dm7 G7 C Am
Please nev - er leave me blue and a - lone, if you ev-er go I'm
Dm7 G7 C Am Dm7 G
sure you'll come back home, be - cause I love you I love you I do,
C Am Dm7 G7 C Am
an - gel ba - by, my an - gel ba - by. It's just like heav - en

Dm7 G7 C Am Dm7 G7
be-in' with you dear, I could nev - er stay a - way with-out you near,
C Am Dm7 G C Am Dm7 G7
be-cause I love you, I love you, I do, an - gel ba - by, my an - gel ba - by.
C Am7 Dm7 G7 C Am Dm7 G7
Ooh, I love you, ooh, I do, no one could love you like I do.
Repeat and Fade
C Em7/B Am Dm7 G7 C Em7/B Am Dm7 G7
Ooh ooh ooh ooh.

BABY, IT'S YOU

Words and Music by MACK DAVID,
BURT BACHARACH and BARNEY WILLIAMS

Moderately
G6/9
Em
G6/9
Sha la la la la la la. Sha la la la la la
mf
Em
G6/9
Em
la. Sha la la la la la la. Sha la la la
C
la. It's not the way you smile that touched my
la. You should hear what they say a - bout
3

G
C
heart. Sha la la la la. It's not the way you kiss
you. Cheat! Cheat! Sha la la la la. They say the way you've
G
that tears me a - part.
nev - er, nev - er, nev - er ev - er been true. Cheat!
Em
Oh, oh, man - y, man - y, man - y nights go by,
Cheat! Oh, oh, it does - n't mat - ter what they say,
Am
I sit a - lone at home and I cry o - ver
I know I'm gon - na love you an - y old way. What can I

G
Em
C
you. What can I do? Can't help my -
do when it's true? Don't want no -
D7
N.C.
G6/9
self
bod - y, no - bod - y,
'cause ba - by, it's you. Sha la la la la la
Em
To Coda
G6/9
1
Em
la. Ba - by, it's you. Sha la la la la la la. Sha la la la
2
Em
C
D
la.
3
3

G
C
D
G
D.S. al Coda
(Verse 1)
Oh, oh,
CODA
G6/9
Em
G6/9
you.
Sha la la la la la la.
Don't leave me all a - lone.
Sha la la la la la
Em
G6/9
Em
G
la.
Come on home.
Sha la la la la la
la.
'Cause, ba - by, it's you.

BIG GIRLS DON'T CRY

Words and Music by BOB CREWE
and BOB GAUDIO

A♭ F7 B♭m7 E♭7 A♭ F7
Big girls don't cry.
(Who said
B♭m7 E♭7 A♭ F7 B♭m7 E♭7
they don't cry?)
My girl said good -
Ba - by, I was
A♭ F7 B♭m7 E♭7 A♭ F7
bye, my, oh my. My girl
cruel, I was cruel. Ba - by,
B♭m7 E♭7 A♭ D♭
did - n't cry. (I won - der
I'm a fool. (I'm such a
4fr

A♭
A♭+
F7
why.) (Sil - ly boy.) Told my girl we
fool.) (Sil - ly girl.) Shame on you, your
B♭7
had to break up. (Sil - ly boy.) Thought that she would
ma - ma said. (Sil - ly girl.) Shame on you, you're
E♭7
call my bluff. (Sil - ly boy.) Then she said, to my sur - prise,
cry'n' in bed. (Sil - ly girl.) Shame on you, you told a lie.
A♭
Cm/E♭
D♭
E♭7
A♭
F7
"Big girls don't do cry." Big girls

B♭m7 E♭7 A♭ F7 B♭m7 E♭7
don't cry, they don't cry.
A♭ F7 B♭m7 E♭7
Big girls don't
1
A♭ F7
cry.
(Who said
B♭m7 E♭7
they don't cry?)
2
A♭ F7 B♭m7 E♭7
cry.
(That's just an al - i - bi.)
A♭ Cm/E♭ D♭ E♭7 A♭ Cm/E♭ D♭ E♭7
4fr 3fr
Big girls don't cry, big girls don't cry.

BOBBY'S GIRL

Words and Music by GARY KLEIN
and HENRY HOFFMAN

C
Am
I know just what to say, I answer
Still in my heart I pray, there soon will
F
Em
right away. There's just one thing I've been wishing for.
come a day when I will have him all to myself.
F6
G7
N.C.
C
I wanna be Bobby's girl,
Am
I wanna be Bobby's girl.

F
G
Dm7
G7
That's the most im - por - tant thing to me.
N.C.
C
And if I was Bob - by's girl; if I was
F
G7
Bob - by's girl, what a faith - ful,
C
1
2
thank - ful girl I'd be.

BUTTERFLY

Words and Music by KAL MANN
and BERNIE LOWE

Moderately
B♭
C7
F
B♭7
mp
F
C7
F
B♭
You tell me you love _ me, you say you'll be true, _ then
F
B♭
you fly a - round _ with some - bod - y new, _ but I'm cra - zy a - bout you,
C7
N.C.
F
B♭7
F
you but - ter - fly. _
You're treat - in' me mean, _ you're

B♭ F B♭
mak - in' me cry, ___ I've made up my mind ___ to tell you good - bye, ___ but I'm
C7 N.C. F B♭
no good with - out you, you but - ter - fly. ___
F7 B♭ F
___ I knew from the first ___ time I kissed you ___ that
B♭ F B♭
you were the trou - bl - in' kind, 'cause the hon - ey drips ___ from

F G7 C7
N.C.
your sweet lips; one taste and I'm out of my mind. I
F B♭ F
love you so much, I know what I'll do; I'm clip - pin' your wings, your
B♭ C7
N.C.
fly - in' is through, 'cause I'm cra - zy a - bout you, you but - ter -
1
F B♭7 F C7
fly. You
2
F B♭7 F
fly.

BOOK OF LOVE

Words and Music by WARREN DAVIS,
GEORGE MALONE and CHARLES PATRICK

Dm
Gm7
C7
I love you, darling, baby, you know I do, but I've
F
Dm
Gm7
C7
F
got to see this book of love, find out why it's true; I wonder, wonder
B♭
F
who, who, who wrote the book of love?
B♭
F
B♭
Chap - ter One says to love her, to love her with all your heart; Chap - ter Two you

C7
F
tell her you're nev - er, nev - er, nev - er, nev - er ev - er gon - na part. In Chap - ter Three re -
Dm
Gm7
C7
F
mem - ber the mean - ing of ro - mance; in Chap - ter Four you
Dm
Gm7
C7
F
break up, but you give her just one more chance. Oh, I won - der, won - der
B♭
F
who, who, who wrote the book of love?

Dm
Gm7
C7
Ba - by, ba - by, ba - by, I love you, yes, I do; well, it
F
Dm
Gm7
C7
says so in this book of love, ours is the one that's true. I
F
B♭
won - der, won - der who, who, who wrote the book of
1
F
love?
2
F
love?
sf

BREAKING UP IS HARD TO DO

Words and Music by HOWARD GREENFIELD
and NEIL SEDAKA

Gm7 C7 F Bm7/E A7 Dm7 G7
mis - er - y. If you go then I'll be blue,
Gm7 Am7 B♭ Gm7 C7 F Dm7
break - ing up is hard to do. Re - mem - ber when you
Gm7 C7 F Dm7 Gm7 C7
held me tight, and you kissed me all through the night,
F Bm7/E A7 Dm7 G7 Gm7 Am7 B♭ C9
think of all that we've been through, break - ing up is hard to

F N.C. Fm7 B♭7 Fm7 B♭7
do. They say that break-ing up is hard to do.
E♭ A♭7 E♭m7 A♭7
Now I know, I know that it's true. Don't say that
E♭m7 A♭7 D♭ C7
this is the end. In-stead of break-ing up I wish that we were mak-ing up a-gain,
D♭7 C7 F Dm7
we were mak-ing up a-gain. I beg of you, don't

Gm7 C9 F Dm7 Dm7/G C9
say good - bye, can't we give our love a brand - new try? Yeah,
F Bm7♭5/E A7♯5 Dm7 Gm7
1
Am7 B♭6 C9
come on, babe, let's start a - new, 'cause break-ing up is hard to do.
F
N.C.
2
Am7 B♭6 C7 Cm6 D7
Don't take your break - ing up is hard to do, 'cause
Gm7 Gm9 C9 C7 F B♭6 F
break - ing up is hard to do.
rit.

BRISTOL STOMP

Words and Music by KAL MANN
and DAVE APPELL

G
Em
C
D
(1., D.S.) The sounds are spin - nin' ev - 'ry Fri - day night.
(2.) It start - ed in Bris - tol at a D. J. hop;
G
Em
C
D
The kids start danc - in' an' they do it right.
they hol - ler and whis - tle, nev - er wan - na stop.
G
Em
C
D
One dance is spe - cial it's a cra - zy sight to
We po - ny and twist - ed and we rocked with dad - dy
G
Em
C
see.
gee.
Kids in Bris - tol 're sharp as a pis - tol when they do the

D G Em
Oh yeah.
Bris - tol Stomp. Real - ly sum - pin' when the joint is jump - in'
C D To Coda C
when they do the Bris - tol Stomp. It's got that
groov - y beat that makes you stomp y'r feet, so
G
come on get in line y'r gon - na feel

C
fine. And when she danc - es with me, we'll fall in
D
C♯
love you'll see, the Bris - tol Stomp - 'll make you
D
D.S. al Coda
mine all mine.
CODA
G
Kids in Bris - tol 're
Em
C
D
Repeat and Fade
sharp as a pis - tol when they do the Bris - tol Stomp.

CALIFORNIA GIRLS

Words and Music by BRIAN WILSON
and MIKE LOVE

Medium Rock
B♭
mf
Well, east coast girls are hip, I real - ly
west coast has the sun - shine, and the
A♭/B♭
E♭
dig those styles they wear; and the south - ern girls with the
girls all get so tanned; I dig a French bi - ki - ni on Ha-
F7
way they talk they knock me out when I'm down there. The
wai - ian is - lands, dolls by a palm tree in the sand. I

B♭
A♭/B♭
Mid - west farm - er's daugh - ters real - ly make you feel al -
been all a - round this great big world, and I've seen all kinds of
E♭
right, and north - ern girls with the way they kiss, they keep their
girls, but I could - n't wait to get back in the states, back to the
F7
B♭
boy - friends warm at night.
cut - est girls in the world.
I wish they all could be
Cm7
A♭
B♭m
Cal - i - for - nia, I wish they all could be Cal - i - for - nia, I

G♭
A♭m
1
B♭
wish they all could be Cal - i - for - nia girls.
2
B♭
The girls.
L.H.
B♭
I wish they all could be
E♭
Repeat and Fade
Cal - i - for - nia, I wish they all could be Cal - i - for - nia... I

CHAPEL OF LOVE

Words and Music by PHIL SPECTOR,
ELLIE GREENWICH and JEFF BARRY

Gm
3fr
C7
F
go - in' to the chap - el of love.
Gm7
F
Gm7
F
C7
F
3
Spring is here, the
Bells will ring, the
C7
F
Gm
3fr
3
sky is blue, whoa, birds will
sun will shine, whoa, I'll be
C7
Gm
3fr
C7
sing as if they knew.
his and he'll be mine.

F C7 F Cm6 D7
3fr
To - day's the day we'll say, "I do."
We'll love un - til the end of time.
And we'll
Gm C7 F C7
3fr
1
nev - er be lone - ly an - y - more. Be - cause we're
2
F C7
D.S. al Coda
more. Be - cause we're
CODA
Gm
3fr
go - in'
Go - in'
to the
Repeat and Fade
Optional Ending
C7 F Gm7 F Gm7 F
chap - el of love.

COME GO WITH ME

Words and Music by
C.E. QUICK

G Em7 Am7 D7 G Em7 Am7 D7
me. Come, come, come, come, come in - to my heart,
G Em7 Am7 D7 G Em7
tell me, dar - lin', we will nev - er part; I need you, dar - lin',
Am7 D7 G C6 G G7 C7
so come go with me. Yes, I need you,
3
G G7
yes, I real - ly need you, please say you'll nev - er leave me.

C7
D7
Well, say you nev - er, yes, you real - ly nev - er, you nev - er give me a
G
Em7
Am7
D7
G
Em7
chance. Come, come, come, come, come in - to my heart, tell me, dar - lin',
Am7
D7
G
Em7
Am7
D7
we will nev - er part; I need you, dar - lin', so come go with
1
G
Em7
Am7
D7
me.
2
G
C6
G
me.
3

DON'T BE CRUEL
(To a Heart That's True)

Words and Music by OTIS BLACKWELL
and ELVIS PRESLEY

Moderately, with half-time feel
N.C.
C
mf
You know I can __ be found __
Ba - by, if I made you mad __
Don't stop think - in' of
Instrumental solo
sit - tin' home all a - lone. __ If
for some - thing I might have __ said, __
me. Don't make me feel this __ way. __ Come
F
C
you can't come __ a - round, at least please tel - e - phone. __
please let's for - get the past. The fu - ture looks bright a - head. __
on o - ver here and love me. You know what I want you to

Dm
G
To Coda
Don't be cruel to a heart that's true.
Don't be cruel to a heart that's true.
say. Don't be cruel to a heart that's true.
C
1
2, 3
(2.) I don't
F
G
F
want no oth - er love. Ba - by, it's just
Why should we be a - part, I real - ly, real - ly love you,
G
C
1
D.S.
(take 2nd ending)
2
N.C.
D.S. al Coda
you I'm think - in' of.
ba - by, cross my heart.

CODA
C
A
Solo ends
Let's
D
walk up to the preach - er.
Let us both say, "I do."
G
Then you'll know you have me and

D
Em7
I know I'll have you, too. Don't be cruel
A
D
Em/A
D
to a heart that's true. I don't
G
A
A♭
4fr
G
want no oth - er love. Ba - by, it's just
A
D
N.C.
you I'm think - in' of. Don't be cruel

Em7
A
D
Em/A
to a heart that's true.
D
Em7
A
Don't you be cruel to a heart that's
D
Em/A
D
Em7
true.
'Said don't you be cruel
A
D
Em/A
Repeat and Fade
D
Optional Ending
D
to a heart that's true.
No, don't be cruel

DANCING IN THE STREET

Words and Music by MARVIN GAYE,
IVY HUNTER and WILLIAM STEVENSON

Moderately, with a steady beat

E7
mf
Call - ing out a - round the world, are you
in - vi - ta - tion a - cross the na - tion, a
read - y for a brand-new beat?
chance for folks to meet.
Sum-mer's here and the
There'll be laugh - ing, sing - ing and
time is right for danc - ing in the street.
mu - sic swing - ing, danc - ing in the street.
They're danc - ing in Chi -
Phil - a - del-phia, P. A.,

ca - go, down in New Or - leans,
Bal - ti - more and D. C., now.
in New York Cit - y.
Can't for - get the Mo - tor Cit - y.
All we need is mu -
A
- sic, sweet mu - sic. There'll be mu - sic ev - 'ry - where.
E7
There'll be swing - ing and sway - ing and rec - ords play - ing,

G♯7
4fr
danc - ing in the street, oh. It does - n't mat - ter what
C♯m
4fr
you wear, just as long as you are there,
F♯m
so come on, ev - 'ry guy grab a girl.
B7sus
2fr
B7
Ev - 'ry - where a - round the world they'll be

E7
(Danc - ing in the street.)
danc - ing, they're danc - ing in the street.
1
2
(Danc - ing in the street.) This is an
Way down in L. A.,
ev - 'ry day they're danc - ing in the street.
get in time, we're danc - ing in the street.
me and you, we're danc - ing in the street.
Repeat and Fade
(Danc - ing in the street.) Let's form a big, strong line,
(Danc - ing in the street.) A - cross the o - cean blue,
(Danc - ing in the street.)

DEDICATED TO THE ONE I LOVE

Words and Music by LOWMAN PAULING
and RALPH BASS

D9
4fr
Em
Bm
cause it's hard for me, my ba - by,
Am7
D7
G
and the dark - est hour is just be - fore dawn.
G7
D7
D9
4fr
Each night be - fore you
(D.S.) I'm far a -
G
Dsus
D7
go to bed,
way from you,
my ba - by,
whis - per a

G
lit - tle prayer for me, my
Dsus
D7
D9
4fr
To Coda I
ba - by. (Yeah)
(1.,3.) And then tell
(2.) Be - cause it's
Gdim7
G
4
all the stars a - bove. This is ded - i -
N.C.
To Coda II
G
cat - ed to the one I love.
Life can nev - er be ex -

act - ly like we want it to be, I could be sat - is -
fied knowing - ing you love me. There's
one thing I want you to do es - pe - cial - ly for
Am
A7
me and it's some - thing that ev - 'ry - bod - y

D9
D7
4fr
D.S. al Coda I
needs.
While
CODA I
Em
Bm
Am7
hard for me, my ba - by,
and the dark - est hour
D7
G7
is just be - fore dawn.
There's
Bm
Em
G
Bm
C
one thing I want you to do
es - pe - cial - ly for

Bm
N.C.
E♭
3fr
me, and it's some - thing ev - 'ry - bod - y
D7
D.S. al Coda II
needs. While
CODA II
Em
Em
Repeat and Fade
C
This is ded - i - cat - ed
love. to the one I love.
This is ded - i -
Optional Ending
C
D7
G
love.

DOWNTOWN

Words and Music by
TONY HATCH

C♯m
E
C♯m
traf - fic in the cit - y. Lin - ger on the side-walk where the ne - on signs are pret - ty.
gen - tle bos - sa no - va. You'll be danc - ing with him, too, be - fore the night is o - ver.
G♯m
A
B/A
A
How can you lose?
Hap - py a - gain.
The lights _ are much bright - er there. You can for -
E/F♯
F♯
E/F♯
F♯
E/B
B6
get all your trou - bles, for - get all your cares, _ so go
down - town.
down - town,
F♯m/B
E/B
B6
F♯m/B
Things-'ll be great _ when you're down - town. No fin - er place _ for sure,
where all the lights _ are bright. Down - town, wait - ing for you _ to - night.

E/B B6 F#m/B
1
E A(add2)/E
Down - town, ev - 'ry - thing's wait - ing for you.
Down - town, you're gon - na be al - right (Down - town.)
B/E A(add2)/E E A(add2)/E B/E A(add2)/E
Down - town.
2
E A(add2)/E E A(add2)/E F B♭(add2)/F
now. Down - town. Down - town.
(Down - town.)
Fsus2 B♭(add2)/F F Fmaj7 B♭/F C/F F Am
Down - town.

B♭ C F Fmaj7 B♭/F C/F F Am
3fr
Down-town.
B♭ C F Dm
Down - town. And you may find some-bod-y kind _ to help and un - der-stand you;
F Dm Am
some-one who is just like you and needs a gen - tle hand to guide them a - long.
B♭ C/B♭ B♭ F/G G
So may - be I'll see you there. We can for - get all our trou - bles, for -

F/G G F/C C6 Gm/C
get all our cares, so go down - town. Things-'ll be great when you're
F/C C6 Gm/C F/C C6
down - town. Don't wait a min - ute more. Down - town.
Gm/C F B♭(add2)/C F B♭(add2)/C F B♭(add2)/C
Ev-'ry-thing's wait - ing for you.
(Down - town.)
Down - town. Down - town.
F B♭(add2)/C
Down - town.
Repeat and Fade
F B♭(add2)/C F B♭(add2)/C
Down - town. Down - town.
Repeat and Fade
F
3fr

EARTH ANGEL

Words and Music by
JESSE BELVIN

E♭ Cm Fm7 B♭7 E♭ Cm
3fr 3fr 3fr 3fr
an - gel, earth an - gel, the one I a - dore, love you for-ev - er and
3 3 3 3
Fm7 B♭7 E♭ Cm Fm7 B♭7
3fr 3fr
ev - er - more. I'm just a fool, a fool in love with
3 3 3
E♭ A♭ E♭ Fm7 E♭7 A♭ A♭m E♭
3fr 4fr 3fr 4fr 4fr 3fr
you. I fell for you, and I knew the
Fm7 B♭7 E♭ E♭7 A♭ Cdim
3fr 4fr 3fr
vi - sion of your love's love - li - ness. I hope and I pray
3

Eb Cm F9 B7 Bb7
3fr 3fr
that some-day I'll be the vi-sion of your hap-pi-ness. Earth
Eb Cm Fm7 Bb7 Eb Cm
3fr 3fr 3fr 3fr
an-gel, earth an-gel, please be mine; my dar-ling, dear,
Fm7 Bb7 Eb Cm Fm7 Bb7
3fr 3fr
love you all the time. I'm just a fool, a fool in love with
1 Eb Cdim Fm7 Bb7
3fr 3fr
you. Earth
2 Eb Fm7 Eb6/9
3fr 5fr
you.

DREAM LOVER

Words and Music by
BOBBY DARIN

Moderately
C
Am
C
Am
C
mf
Ev - 'ry night I hope and pray
Am
C
a dream lov - er will come my way,
a girl to hold
in my arms
Am
and know the mag - ic of her charms. Be - cause I

C
G7
C
want a girl to call my
F
C
Am
Dm7
G7sus
G7
own. I want a dream lov - er so I don't have to dream a - lone.
C
G7
C
Dream lov - er,
Dream lov - er,
Am
where are you, with a love, oh, so true,
un - til then, I'll go to sleep and dream a - gain.

C
Am
and a hand that I can hold
to feel you near when
That's the on - ly thing to do
un - til my lov - er's
C
G7
I grow old?
dreams come true.
Be - cause I want
a girl
to
C
F
C
Am
call my own,
I want a dream
lov - er so
To Coda
Dm7
G7sus
G7
C
C7
I don't have to dream a - lone.

F
F7
C
Some - day, I don't know how, I hope you'll
D7
hear my plea. Some way, I don't know how,
G7
D.S. al Coda
she'll bring her love to me.
CODA
C

DUKE OF EARL

Words and Music by EARL EDWARDS,
EUGENE DIXON and BERNICE WILLIAMS

E♭
3fr
Cm
3fr
I'm gon - na love you,
I'm gon - na love you,
A♭
4fr
let me hold you, 'cause I'm the Duke of
let me hold you, 'cause I'm the Duke of
1
B♭
Earl.
2
B♭
Earl.
E♭
3fr
Cm
3fr
A♭
4fr
B♭
E♭
3fr

EV'RYBODY'S SOMEBODY'S FOOL
(Everybody's Somebody's Fool)

Words and Music by JACK KELLER
and HOWARD GREENFIELD

F
though you on - ly lead me on and hurt me, I
dar - ling, I'd be twice as blue with - out you. It
C
G7
C
could - n't bring my - self to say good - bye.
hurts, but I'd come run - ning back for more.
'Cause
F
ev - 'ry - bod - y's some - bod - y's fool,
G7
F/C
C
ev - 'ry - bod - y's some - bod - y's play - thing and

F
there are no ex - cep - tions to the rule. Yes,
C
G7
To Coda
1
C
ev - 'ry - bod - y's some - bod - y's fool.
2
C
I fool. Some -
F
day you'll find some - one to real - ly care for and

G7
C
if her love should prove to be un - true, you'll
F
know how much this heart of mine is break - ing, you'll
C
G7
C
cry for her the way I cried for you.
D.S. al Coda
Yes,
CODA
C
fool.

GET A JOB

Words and Music by EARL BEAL, RICHARD LEWIS,
RAYMOND EDWARDS and WILLIAM HORTON

Moderately, with a rockin' beat

G7 F G C
To Coda
yip yip yip yip yip yip yip yip, mum mum mum mum mum mum. Get a job, sha da da da
Dm7 C F C
sha da da da da. Ev - 'ry morn - ing a - bout this time she get me out of my bed a - cry - ing get a
3
F
job. Af - ter break - fast ev - 'ry day, she throws the
G7
want ads right my way and nev - er fails to say, get a

C
job. Sha da da da sha da da da da, sha da da da
sha da da da da, F
sha da da da sha da da da da,
C
sha da da da sha da da da da, G7
yip yip yip yip yip yip yip yip,
F G C
mum mum mum mum mum mum. Get a job, sha da da da sha da da da da, and

F
C
when I get the paper, I read it through and through and
D7
G7
my {girl / wife} never fails to say if there is any work for me.
C
And when I go back to the house I
hear the woman's mouth preaching and a-crying, tell me that I'm lying 'bout a

G7
C
D.S. al Coda
job that I nev - er could find. Sha da da da
CODA
sha da da da da, sha da da da sha da da da da,
sha da da da sha da da da da, sha da da da
sha da da da da, sha da da da sha da da da da.

GOIN' OUT OF MY HEAD

Words and Music by TEDDY RANDAZZO
and BOBBY WEINSTEIN

E♭ Gm E♭ Gm
want you to want me I need you so bad - ly, I
see you each morn - ing; but you just walk past me, you
A♭ B♭7 Fm7 Cmaj7
can't think of an - y - thing but you. And I
don't e - ven know that I ex -
Cmaj7 Dm7 G7 Cmaj7 Dm7
ist. Go - in' out of my head o - ver you, out of my
Cmaj7 Dm7 C F6 C
head o - ver you. Out of my head day and night,

F6 C F6 C F6 C
night and day and night, wrong or right, I must think of a
D Fm6 C Cdim
way into your heart, there's no rea-son
G G7 F♯dim G
why my be-ing shy should keep us a-part.
Cm7 Cmaj7
Repeat and Fade
And I think I'm go-ing out of my head. Yes, I

GOODNIGHT, SWEETHEART, GOODNIGHT
(Goodnight, It's Time to Go)

Words and Music by JAMES HUDSON
and CALVIN CARTER

With a slow beat

G Em Am D7 G Em
Good-night, sweet-heart, well, it's time to go. Good-night, sweet-heart, well, it's
Am D7 G G7/B C Cm
3fr
time to go. I hate to leave you, but I real-ly must say, good-
G/D Am7 D7 G G7 C Cm
3fr
night, sweet - heart, good - night.
Well, it's three o' - clock in the
Now, my moth - er and my
G G7 C G/D Am7 G G7
morn - ing, ba - by, I just can't treat you right. Well, I
fa - ther might hear if I stay here too long. One
3
3

C Cm G F9 E7 A7
hate to leave you, ba - by, don't mean may - be, be - cause I love you
kiss and we'll part, and you'll be go - ing. You know I hate to see you
D7 G Em Am D7
so.
go.
Good - night, sweet - heart, well, it's time to go.
G Em Am D7 G G7/B
Good - night, sweet - heart, well, it's time to go. I hate to leave you, but I
C Cm G/D Am7 D7 G6 E9 E♭9 D9 G6 A♭7 G6/9
real - ly must say, good - night, sweet - heart, good - night. night.

HEATWAVE
(Love Is Like a Heatwave)

Words and Music by EDWARD HOLLAND,
LAMONT DOZIER and BRIAN HOLLAND

Moderately fast
Eb Ab/Eb Eb Ab/Eb Ab/Eb Eb Ab/Eb Eb Ab/Eb Eb Ab/Eb
mf
Eb N.C. Fm7 Gm7
When - ev - er I'm with him, some - thing in -
calls my name, soft,
stare in space, tears all
yeah, yeah, yeah, whoa
Cm7 Fm7
side starts to burn - in'
low, sweet and plain, I feel, yeah,
o - ver my face. I can't ex - plain it don't un - der -
ho. Yeah, yeah, yeah,

Gm7
Cm7
and I'm filled with de - sire.
yeah, well, I feel that burn - in' flame. Has
stand it, I ain't nev - er felt like this be - fore. Now
yeah, ho, yeah.
Fm7
Gm7
A♭6
Could it be a dev - il in me or is this the way love's sup -
high blood pres - sure got a hold on me or is this the way love's sup -
that fun - ny feel - in' has me a - mazed; I don't know what to do, my
Don't pass up this chance; this time it's a
B♭7
E♭
A♭
E♭
A♭
E♭
A♭
E♭
A♭
3fr
4fr
3fr
4fr
3fr
4fr
3fr
4fr
posed to be?
posed to be?
head's in a haze.
true ro - mance.
It's like a heat - wave burn - in' in my

Eb Ab Eb Ab Eb Ab Eb Ab Eb Ab Eb Ab
3fr 4fr
heart. I can't keep from cry - in',
Eb Ab Eb Ab Eb Ab Eb Ab
it's tear - in' me a - part.
1-3
Eb
N.C.
When - ev - er he
Some - times I
Yeah, yeah, yeah,
4
Eb
N.C.
Fm7
Gm7
Ab6
Bb7
Eb

HAPPY BIRTHDAY SWEET SIXTEEN

Words and Music by HOWARD GREENFIELD
and NEIL SEDAKA

Em
G7
because you're not a baby any-
more.
C
C♯dim
4fr
You've turned into the prettiest
G
E7
A7
girl I've ever seen.
Happy
D7
birthday, sweet sixteen.

G
B7
What hap - pened to that fun - ny face?
Em
My lit - tle tom - boy now wears
G7
C
sat - ins and lace. I can't be -
C♯dim7
G
E7
lieve my eyes, you're just a teen - age dream.

A7
D7
G
Hap - py birth - day, sweet six - teen.
D7
G
When you were on - ly six,
I was your big broth - er.
D7
G
Then when you were ten,
we did - n't like each
E7
oth - er.
When you were thir - teen,
you were my

Am
A7
fun - ny val - en - tine. But since you've grown up, your
D7
Am
D7
fu - ture is sewn up, from now on you're gon - na be mine. So
G
B7
if I should smile with sweet sur - prise,
Em
G7
it's just that you've grown up be - fore my ver - y eyes.

C
C♯dim
4fr
G
E7
You've turned in - to the pret - ti - est girl I've ev - er seen.
A7
D7
1
G
Am7
D7
Hap - py birth - day, sweet six - teen.
2
G
Am7
D7
G
Em
teen.
Tra la la la la la la la la. Hap-py
C
D7
Play 3 times
G
birth - day, sweet six - teen.

HELP ME RHONDA

Words and Music by BRIAN WILSON
and MIKE LOVE

B♭
G7
fine, ___ and I know it would-n't take much time ___ for you to
eye, ___ and I'll give you lots of rea - sons why ___ you got - ta
F
C7
F
help me, Rhon - da, help me get her out of my heart. _
C7
F
Help me, Rhon - da! Help, help me, Rhon - da! Help me, Rhon - da! Help, help me, Rhon - da!
C7
F
Help me, Rhon - da! Help, help me, Rhon - da! Help me, Rhon - da! Help, help me, Rhon - da!

B♭
Dm
F
Help me, Rhon - da! Help, help me, Rhon - da! Help me, Rhon - da! Help, help me, Rhon - da!
Gm7
C9
1
F
Help me, Rhon - da! Yeah, get her out of my heart.
She was
2
F
C7
Help me, Rhon - da! Help, help me, Rhon - da!
F
Repeat and Fade
Optional Ending
Help me, Rhon - da! Help, help me, Rhon - da!

I GET AROUND

Words and Music by BRIAN WILSON
and MIKE LOVE

Medium bright Rock beat
C
A7
I get a - round from town to town.
mf
Dm
C
I'm a real cool head, I'm mak - in' real good bread.
B♭
G7
N.C.
I'm get - tin' bugged driv - in' up an' down the
al - ways take my car 'cause it's

same ol' strip, I got - ta find a new place where the kids are hip.
nev - er been beat and we've nev - er missed yet with the girls we meet.
My bud - dies and me are get - tin'
None of the guys go stead - y 'cause it
real well - known, yeah, the bad guys know us and they leave us a - lone.
would - n't be right to leave your best girl home on a Sat - ur - day night.
I get a -
C
A7
round from town to town.

Dm
C
B♭
I'm a real cool head, I'm mak-in' real good bread.
1
G7
2
G7
C
We I get a - round from town to
A7
Dm
town. I'm a real cool head,
C
B♭
G7
Repeat and Fade
Optional Ending
C
I'm mak-in' real good bread. I get a - round.

HEY PAULA

Words and Music by
RAY HILDEBRAND

G Am7 G D7 G Em
love, my love. She: Hey! Paul, I've been
3
Am7 D7 G Em7 Am7 D7
wait - ing for you. Hey! Hey! Hey! Paul, I wan - na mar - ry you, too, if
G Em G Em7 Am7
you love me true, if you love me still. Our love will al - ways be
Am7/D D7 G Am7 G D7
5fr
real, my love, my love.
3 3

G Em7 Am7 D7 Am7 D7
Both: True love means plan - ning a life for two, be - ing to - geth - er the
G E7 Am
whole day through. True love means wait - ing and hop - ing that soon
A7 Am7/D D7 G Am7
wish - es we've made will come true, my love, my
G D7 G Em7 Am7 D7
love. He: Hey! Hey! Paul - a, I've been wait - ing for you. She: Hey! Hey!

G Em7 Am7 D7 G Em7
Paul, I want to mar - ry you, too. Both: True love means plan - ning a
Am7 D7 Am7 D7 G
life for two, be - ing to - geth - er the whole day through.
E7 Am A7
True love means wait - ing and hop - ing that soon wish - es we've made will come
Am7/D D7 G Am7 G A♭9♯11 G6/9
true, my love, my love.
molto rit.

I WILL FOLLOW HIM
(I Will Follow You)

English Words by NORMAN GIMBEL and ARTHUR ALTMAN
French Words by JACQUES PLANTE
Music by J.W. STOLE and DEL ROMA

E♭ Cm N.C. E♭
way. I must fol - low him.
Gm
Ev - er since he touched my hand I knew that
Cm Gm A♭
near him I al - ways must be, and noth - ing can keep him from
B♭7 E♭ B♭7
me, he is my des - ti - ny. I

E♭
3fr
Cm
3fr
love him, I love him, I love him and where he goes I'll fol - low,
I'll fol - low, I'll
for - ev - er and
Fm7
B♭7
E♭
3fr
fol - low. He'll al - ways be my true love, my true love, my true love, from now un - til for -
ev - er and side by side to - geth - er I'll be with my true love, and share a thou - sand
Cm
3fr
N.C.
E♭
3fr
ev - er, for - ev - er, for - ev - er.
sun - sets to - geth - er be - side him.
I will fol - low him,
Gm
3fr
fol - low him wher - ev - er he may go.
There

Cm Gm A♭
is - n't an o - cean too deep, a moun - tain so high it can
Fm7 B♭7 E♭
keep, keep me a - way,
1
E♭/B♭ B♭7 E♭
a - way from my love.
B♭7
I
2
Fm7 B♭7 E♭
a - way from my love.
Ah.
Cm E♭
3fr
4fr
6fr

I WONDER WHY

Words and Music by MELVIN ANDERSON
and RICARDO WEEKS

B♭
C7
To Coda
1
F
why I love you like I do, like I do.
why they think that we will part, we will
why I'm sure you're al - ways true, al - ways
Gm7
C7
2 F
part.
B♭
F
F7
3
3
B♭
Bong! Bong! Bong! Bong!
Ooh

F
F7
ooh.
B♭
Bong! Bong! Bong! Bong!
C7
D.S. al Coda
Bop bop bop bop bop bop bop.
CODA
F
Gm7
C7
F
true.

IT'S ALL IN THE GAME

Lyrics by CARL SIGMAN
Music by CHARLES GATES DAWES

F6 G7
words with him and your fu - ture's look - ing
C Fm C E♭dim Dm7 G7
dim, but these things your hearts can rise a -
C7 E♭dim C7 F
bove. Once in a while he won't call, but it's
3 3
Gm7 C7 F C7
all in the game. Soon he'll be there at your
3 3

F Gm7 B♭/C F
side with a sweet bou - quet.
F6
And he'll kiss your lips and ca -
Am7 Dm7 G7 F C9 C7
ress your wait - ing fin - ger - tips, and your hearts will fly a -
1 F C7 2 F6 F6/9
way. Man - y a tear has to way.
3 3 3 3 3 3

I'M SORRY

Words and Music by RONNIE SELF
and DUB ALBRITTEN

Slowly
C
B7
C
A♭13
4fr
G7
mp
C
B7
C
C♯dim7
I'm sor - ry, so sor - ry, that I was such a fool.
Dm7
G7
Dm7
G7
C
C♯dim7
Dm7
G7♯5
I did - n't know love could be so cruel.
C
B7
C
C♯dim7
You tell me mis - takes are part of be - ing young, but

Dm7 G7 Dm7 G7 C C♯dim7 Dm7 G7♯5
that does-n't right the wrong that's been done.
C B7 C
I'm sor-ry, so sor-ry; please ac-cept my
C♯dim7 Dm7 G7 Dm7 G7
a-pol-o-gy, but love is blind and I was too blind to
C A♭13 4fr G7 C F7 C
see. see.
rall.

IN THE STILL OF THE NITE
(I'll Remember)

Words and Music by
FRED PARRIS

C
Am
love, love you so, promise I'll
F
Dm7
G7
nev - er let you go, in the still of the
C
F
C
C7
nite. I re -
F
mem - ber that nite in May, the

C
G+
3fr
C
G7
C7
stars were bright a - bove. I'll
F
hope and I'll pray to
G7
keep your pre - cious love.
Well,
So,
be -
C
Am
fore the light, hold me a -

F Dm7 G7
gain, with all of your might, in the still of the
1
C F Dm7 G7
nite. In the
2
C F Dm7 G7
nite. In the still of the
C F C
nite.

IT'S MY PARTY

Words and Music by HERB WIENER,
WALLY GOLD and JOHN GLUCK, JR.

Moderately
C
C+
F
f
G7
C
E♭
3fr
No - bod - y knows where my John - ny has gone, but
Play all my rec - ords, keep danc - ing all night, but
Ju - dy and John - ny just walked through the door,
C
F
A♭
4fr
Ju - dy left the same time. Why was he
leave me a - lone for a while. 'Til John - ny's
like a queen with her king. Oh, what a

C
D7
G7
hold - ing her hand, when he's sup - posed to be mine?
danc - ing with me, I've got no rea - son to smile.
birth - day sur - prise; Ju - dy's wear - ing his ring.
C
C+
F
It's my par - ty, and I'll cry if I want to, cry if I want to,
Fm
C
G7
cry if I want to. You would cry, too, if it hap - pened to
C
F
C
1, 2
G7
3
G7
C
you.

JUDY'S TURN TO CRY

Words and Music by BEVERLY ROSS
and EDNA LEWIS

Moderately bright
B♭ B♭+ E♭ Cm
f
A♭ B♭ E♭ B♭7
When Ju - dy left with John - ny at my par - ty, and
hurt me so to see them dance to - geth - er, I
night I saw them kiss - ing at a par - ty, so
E♭ B♭7 E♭
came back wear - ing his ring, I sat down and cried my
felt like mak - ing a scene. Then my tears just fell like
I kissed some oth - er guy. John - ny jumped up and

E
A
B♭
B♭
B♭+
eyes out, now that was a fool - ish thing. 'Cause now it's
rain - drops, 'cause Ju - dy's smile was so mean. But now it's
hit him, 'cause he still loved me, that's why. So now it's
E♭
Cm
Ju - dy's turn to cry, Ju - dy's turn to cry, Ju - dy's turn to cry,
A♭
B♭
'cause John-ny's come back to me.
E♭
1, 2
B♭7
3
B♭7
E♭
It
One
3fr
4fr

LEADER OF THE PACK

Words and Music by GEORGE MORTON,
JEFF BARRY and ELLIE GREENWICH

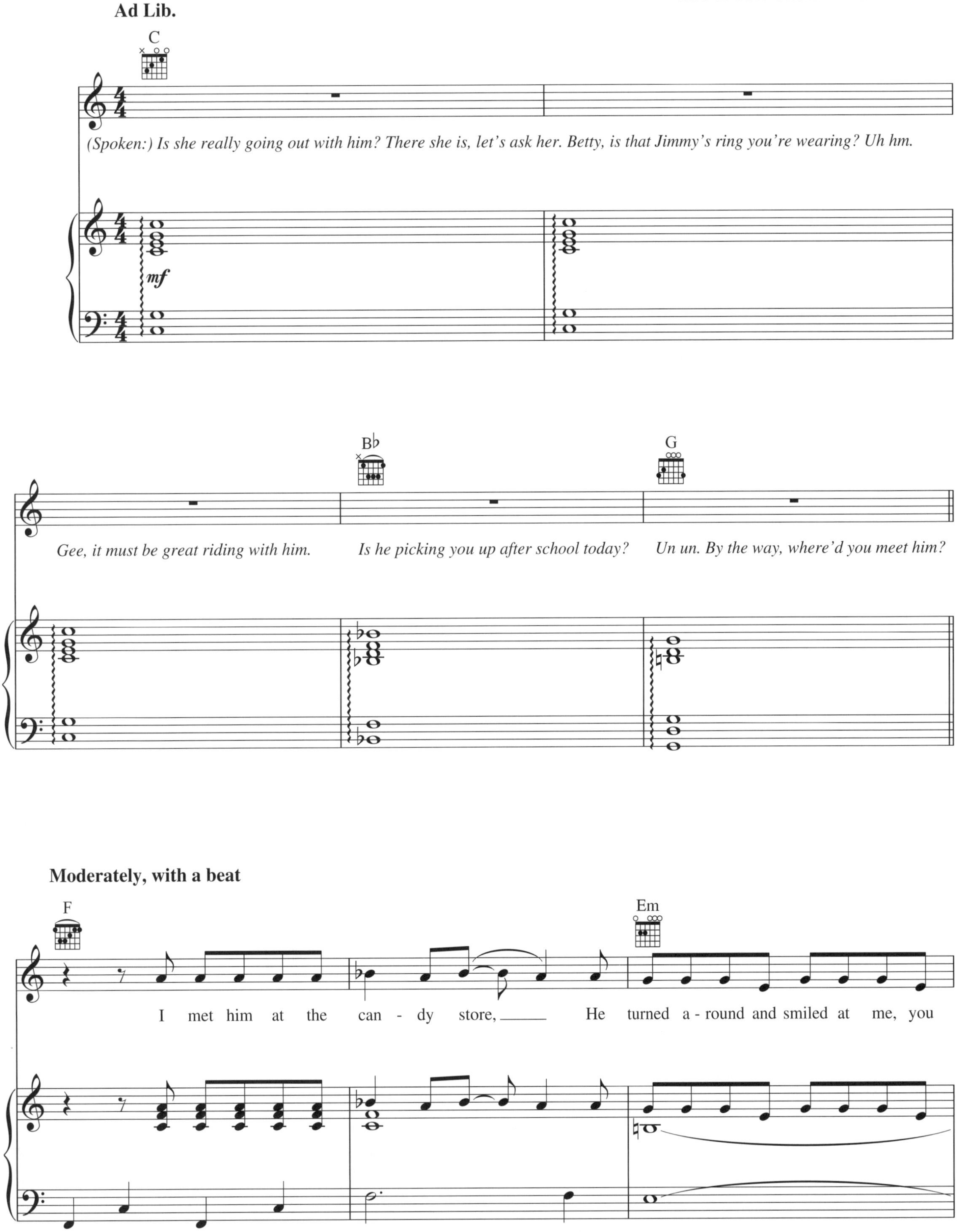
Ad Lib.
C
(Spoken:) Is she really going out with him? There she is, let's ask her. Betty, is that Jimmy's ring you're wearing? Uh hm.
mf
B♭
G
Gee, it must be great riding with him.
Is he picking you up after school today?
Un un. By the way, where'd you meet him?
Moderately, with a beat
F
Em
I met him at the can - dy store, He turned a - round and smiled at me, you

G7
get the pic - ture? Yes, we see. That's when I fell for the lead - er of the
C
pack.
C
My folks were
One day my
I felt so
al - ways put - ting him down.
dad said find some - one new.
help - less, what could I do?
3
Bb
They said he came from the wrong side of town.
I had to tell my Jim - my we're through.
Re - mem - b'ring all the things we'd been through.

G
To Coda
F
They told me he was bad,
He stood there and asked me why,
Em
G7
But I know he was sad,
That's why I
But all I could do was cry,
I'm sor - ry I
fell for the lead - er of the
hurt you, the lead - er of the
1
C
pack.
2
C
Bm
Am
pack.
(Spoken:) He sort of smiled and kissed me goodbye,

But the tears were beginning to show as he drove away
on that rainy night.
I begged him to go slow,
D.S. al Coda
but whether he heard, I'll never know.
CODA
F
In school they all
stop and stare,
Em
I can't hide the tears, but I don't care.
G7
I'll nev - er for - get him, the lead - er of the
C
pack.

LET IT BE ME
(Je t'appartiens)

English Words by MANN CURTIS
French Words by PIERRE DeLANOE
Music by GILBERT BECAUD

Relaxed
F C A/C♯ B♭/D Gm/B♭ Gm7
mf
C7sus C7 F C/E C C♯dim7
I bless the day I found you,
If, for each bit of glad - ness,
Dm Am/C B♭
I want to stay a - round you, and so I
some - one must taste of sad - ness, I'll bear the
F/A Gm7 B♭/C C7♭9 F Gm7 C7
beg you, let it be me.
sor - row, let it be me.

F
C/E
C
C♯dim7
Dm
Don't take this heav - en from one, if you must
No mat - ter what the price is, I'll make the
Am/C
B♭
F/A
cling to some - one, now and for - ev - er,
sac - ri - fic - es, through each to - mor - row,
Gm7
B♭/C
C7♭9
F
B♭
let it be me. Each time we
let it be me. To you I'm
Am
B♭
F
meet, love, I find com - plete love,
pray - ing, hear what I'm say - ing,

Gm7
F/A
B♭
with - out your sweet love, what would life
please let your heart beat for me, just
A
F
C/E
C
C♯dim7
be? So
me. And
nev - er leave me lone - ly,
Dm
Am/C
B♭
tell me you'll love me on - ly, and that you'll
F/A
Gm7
B♭/C
C7♭9
1 F
Gm7/C
C7
2 F
al - ways let it be me. me.

LIMBO ROCK

Words and Music by BILLY STRANGE
and JON SHELDON

Moderately slow Calypso

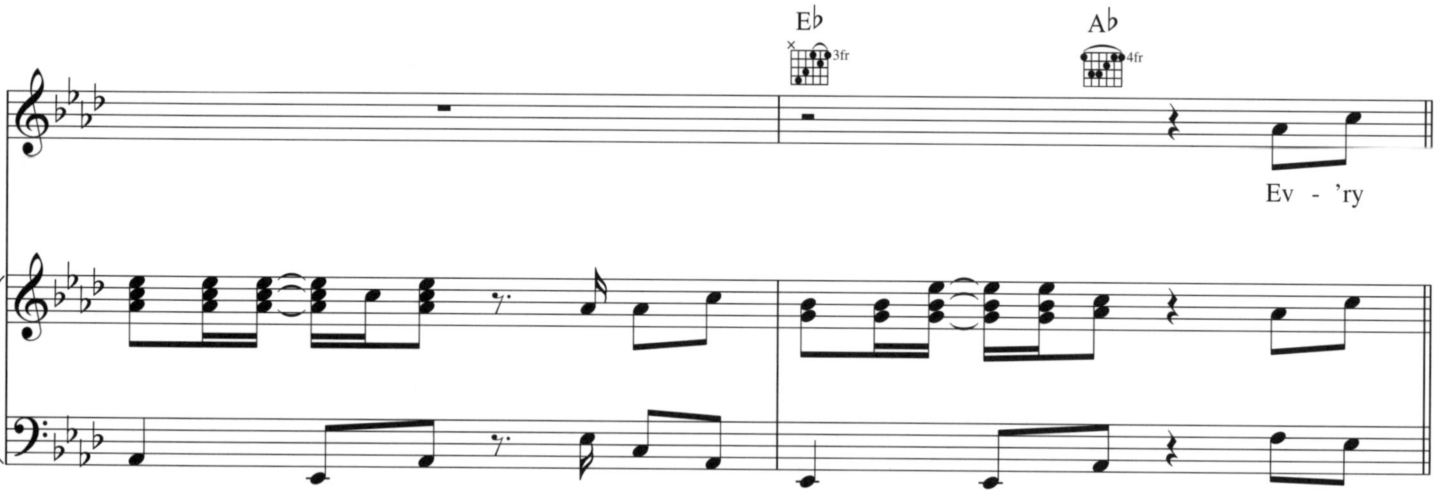

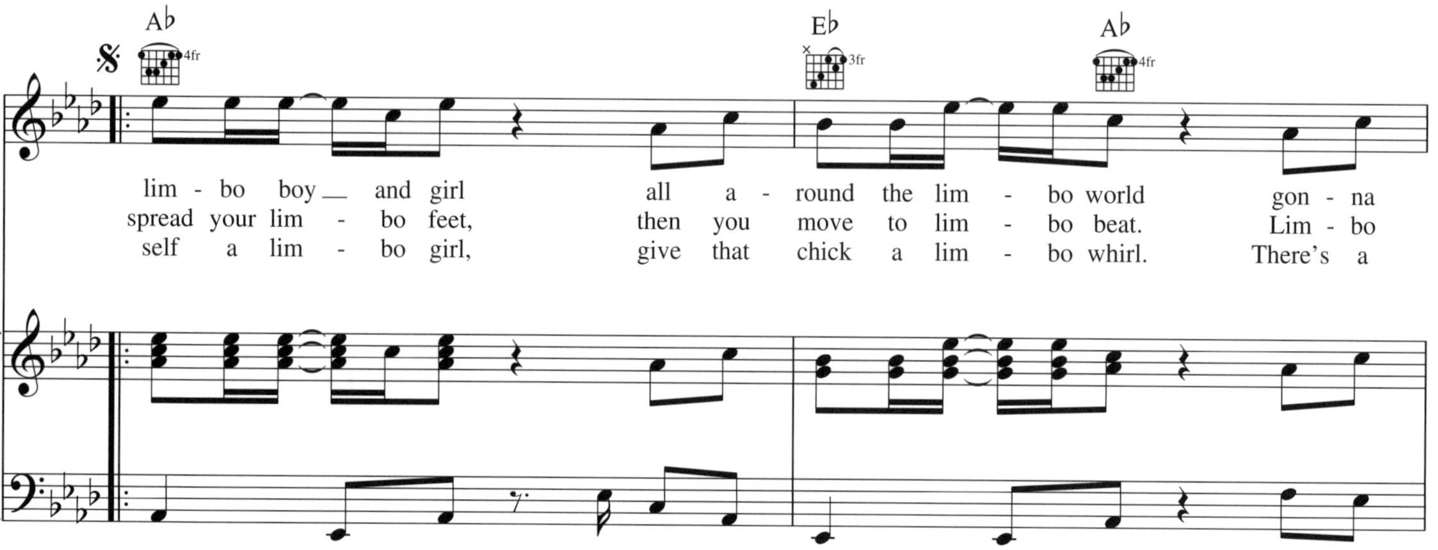

E♭
A♭
do the lim - bo rock all a - round the lim - bo block.
an - kle, lim - bo knee, bend back like a lim - bo tree.
lim - bo moon a - bove, you will fall in lim - bo love.
Jack be
D♭
A♭
E♭
lim - ber, Jack be quick, Jack go un - der lim - bo stick. All a -
To Coda
1
A♭
D♭
A♭
N.C.
round the lim - bo clock, hey let's do the lim - bo rock.
(Spoken:) Limbo lower now,
limbo
Percussion:

lower now. How low can you go? First, you
2
A♭ D♭ A♭
do the lim - bo rock. La, la, la, la, la, la, la, la; la, la, la,
E♭ A♭
la, la, la, la, la; la, la, la, la, la, la, la, la; la, la, la,
E♭ A♭ D♭
la, la, la, la, la; la, la, la, la, la, la, la, la; la, la, la,
4fr
3fr

A♭
E♭
la, la, la,___ la, la; la, la, la, la, la, la,___ la, la; la, la, la,
A♭
D♭
A♭
D.S. al Coda
la, la, la,___ la, la. Get your -
CODA
A♭
D♭
A♭
N.C.
do the lim - bo rock.
(Spoken:) Don't move that limbo bar. You'll be a limbo star.
Percussion:
How low can you go?
La, la, la,

A♭
4fr
E♭
3fr
A♭
4fr
la, la, la, la, la; la, la, la, la, la, la, la, la; la, la, la,
E♭
3fr
A♭
4fr
la, la, la, la, la; la, la, la, la, la, la, la, la; la, la, la,
D♭
A♭
4fr
E♭
3fr
la, la, la, la, la; la, la, la, la, la, la, la, la; la, la, la,
A♭
4fr
D♭
A♭
4fr
la, la, la, la, la; la, la, la, la, la, la, la, la.

LIPSTICK ON YOUR COLLAR

Words by EDNA LEWIS
Music by GEORGE GOEHRING

Moderate Rock beat
B♭ D7 Gm C7 F7
f
B♭ Gm Cm7
When you left me all a - lone at the Rec - ord
You said it be - longed to me; made me stop and
mp
F7 Cm7 F7 B♭ Gm
Hop, told me you were go - in' out
think, then I no - ticed yours was red,
Cm7 F7 Cm7 F7 B♭
for a so - da pop. You were gone for
mine was ba - by pink. You walked in with

B♭7
E♭
3fr
C7
quite a while, half an hour or more. You came back and
Mar - y Jane, lip - stick all a mess. Were you smooch - in'
F7
B♭
man, oh man, this is what I saw:
my best friend? Guess the an - swer's yes.
Lip - stick on your
E♭
3fr
B♭
col - lar told a tale on you. Lip - stick on your
E♭
3fr
col - lar said you were un - true.

B♭
D7
Gm
Bet your bot - tom dol - lar
you and I are
Dm
E♭
B♭
through 'cause lip - stick on your col - lar
F7
Cm
F7
1
B♭
2
B♭
told a tale on you.
you.
F7
Cm
F7
B♭
F7
Cm
F7
B♭
Told a tale on you.
Told a tale on you.
3fr

LITTLE BITTY PRETTY ONE

Words and Music by
ROBERT BYRD

Mm.
Mm.
Mm.
Oh.
Oh.
Oh.

Oh.
(1.,3.) Lit - tle bit - ty
(2.,4.) I can tell you a
F
pret - ty one,
come on and talk to me.
sto - ry,
hap - pened a long time a - go.
Lov - ey dov - ey love - ly one,
come sit down on my knee.
Lit - tle bit - ty pret - ty one,
I've been watch - ing you grow.
1, 2

3
Bm.
Bm.
Bm.
(Spoken:) Come on, everybody.
Let's put our hands
Bm.
together
and
sing along.
4

Oh.
Oh.
Oh.
Repeat and Fade
Oh.

LITTLE DARLIN'

Words and Music by
MAURICE WILLIAMS

Gm
3fr
I was wrong to
3
Cm7
3fr
F7
try to love _ two,
B♭6
know - ing well that my
Gm
3fr
Cm7
3fr
love was _ just
3

(Spoken over repeat:) (optional)

My dear, I need your love to call my own
And never do wrong; and to hold in mine your little hand.
I'll know too soon that I'll love again.
Please come back to me.

THE LITTLE OLD LADY
(From Pasadena)

Words and Music by DON ALTFELD
and ROGER CHRISTIAN

C
white gar - de - nias.
nev - er lose her.
four - two - six now.
(Go, Gran - ny, go, Gran - ny,
G7
C7
F
go, Gran - ny, go.)
But parked in a rick - et - y
She's gon - na get a tick - et now,
The guys come to race her from
B♭
G
E♭
3fr
C
old gar - age, there's a brand - new shin - y su - per - stocked Dodge.
soon - er or lat - er, 'cause she can't keep her foot off the ac - cel - er - a - tor.
miles a - round, but she'll give 'em a length, then she'll shut 'em down.
F
And ev - 'ry - bod - y's say - in' that there's no - bod - y mean - er than the

B♭7
lit - tle old la - dy from Pas - a - de - na. She drives real fast and she
F
drives real hard. She's the ter - ror of Col - o - ra - do Bou - le - vard. It's the
A♭
4fr
C7
1, 2
lit - tle old la - dy from Pas - a - de - na!
If you
You'll
3
F
Repeat and Fade
The lit - tle old la - dy from Pas - a - de - na. The

LITTLE STAR

Words and Music by ARTHUR VENOSA
and VITO PICONE

Gm7
Cm7
F7
Last time, To Coda
ra ta ta ta tu.
B♭
Gm7
Cm7
Twin - kle, twin - kle lit - tle star, how I won - der
high a - bove the clouds some - where, send me down a
F7
B♭
F7
B♭
where you are, Oh.
love to share.
N.C.
E♭
Oh, there you are, high a -

1
B♭
bove;
oh
God,
send me a
love.
2
F7
I need a love,
oh
D.S. (vs. 1 & 2) al Coda
me, oh me, oh my.
CODA
Slowly
B♭
Oh, ra ta ta
Freely
E♭
3fr
F7
B♭
oh.
There you are, lit - tle star.

MY GUY

Words and Music by
WILLIAM "SMOKEY" ROBINSON

Cm F6 Cm F6 Cm F6
stick - ing to my guy like a stamp to a let - ter, like birds of a feath - er we
gave my guy my word of hon - or to be faith - ful,
Cm B♭ B♭maj7
stick to - geth - er. I'm tell - in' you from the start I can't
and I'm gon - na. You best be be - liev - ing I won't
C7 F6 B♭
be torn a - part from my guy.
be de - ceiv - ing my guy.
1 Cm Dm
2 Cm Dm Cm7 F
As a mat - ter of o - pin - ion I

Cm F Cm F B♭
think he's tops. My o - pin - ion is he's the cream of the crop. As a
Gm/F Dm Gm/F Dm C7
mat - ter of taste to be ex - act he's my i - deal as a
F7 B♭maj7 B♭6 B♭maj7 B♭6
mat - ter of fact. No mus - cle - bound man could take my hand from my
take my hand
B♭maj7 B♭6 B♭maj7 B♭6 B♭maj7 B♭6
guy. (My guy.) No hand - some face could ev - er

B♭maj7 B♭6 Dm D7
take the place of my guy. (My guy.) He
Cm F Cm F Cm F
may not be a mov - ie star, but when it comes to be - in' hap - py
To Coda
Cm B♭ Gm C7 F7
we are. There's not a man to - day who could take me a - way from my
B♭maj7 B♭6 Cm Dm B♭
guy.
3fr

Cm
Dm
D.S. al Coda
No
CODA
B♭
Gm
C7
F7
man to - day who could take me a - way from my
B♭maj7
B♭6
Repeat and Fade
Cm
Dm
guy.
(Spoken:) What you say, tell me more.
There's not a
Optional Ending
Cm
Dm
B♭
(Instrumental)

LONELY TEARDROPS

Words and Music by BERRY GORDY,
GWEN GORDY FUQUA and TYRAN CARLO

F7
N.C.
home, come home. Just say you
B♭
will, say you will, say you
Gm
E♭
will. Hey hey.
B♭
Cm7
B♭
E♭
My heart is cry - in', cry - in'. Lone - ly tear - drops,

E♭m
6fr
B♭
my pil - low's nev - er dry.
Lone - ly
tear - drops, come home, come
F7
N.C.
home.
Just say you will, say you
B♭
Gm
3fr
will, say you will.
Hey

E♭
B♭
hey.
Just
B♭9
B♭7
E♭
give me an - oth - er chance for
E♭m
B♭
our ro - mance, come on and tell me
D7
that one day you'll re - turn, 'cause

E♭
E♭m
ev - 'ry day that you've been gone a -
F7
B♭
way, you'll know how my heart does noth - ing but burn.
B♭
E♭
Cry - in' lone - ly tear - drops, my pil - low's
E♭m
B♭
nev - er dry. Lone - ly tear - drops, come

F7
N.C.
home, come home. Just say you
B♭
will, say you will, say you
Gm
3fr
B♭
will. Hey hey, say it right now,
Gm
3fr
B♭
ba - by. Come on, come on.

MY BOYFRIEND'S BACK

Words and Music by ROBERT FELDMAN,
GERALD GOLDSTEIN and RICHARD GOTTEHRER

G
C
(Hey la, hey
You've been spread - in' lies that I was un - true,
gon - na be sor - ry you ev - er were born,
D7
G
la, my boy-friend's back.)
so look out now 'cause he's com - in' af - ter you.
'cause he's kind of big and he's aw - ful strong.
C
D7
G
(Hey la, hey la, my boy-friend's back.)
And he
And he
C
D7
G
C
D7
knows that you've been try - in', and he knows that you've been ly - in'.
knows a - bout you cheat - in'. Now you're gon - na get a beat - in'.

C
(Wah -
What made you think he'd be - lieve all your lies?
G
C
ooh Wah - ooh)
You're a big man now, but he'll
G
A
D
(Wah - ooh)
cut you down to size!
Wait and see!
My
G
boy - friend's back, he's gon - na save my rep - u - ta - tion.

C
D7
(Hey la, hey la, my boy - friend's back.)
If
G
I were you I'd take a per - ma - nent va - ca - tion.
C
D7
G
(Hey la, hey la, my boy-friend's back.)
La, hey
C
D7
G
C
D7
Repeat and Fade
la, my boy-friend's back! La, hey la, my boy-friend's back!

ON BROADWAY

Words and Music by BARRY MANN, CYNTHIA WEIL,
MIKE STOLLER and JERRY LEIBER

Moderately, with a beat
F
E♭/F
They say the ne - on lights are bright on
They say the girls are some - thin' else on
They say that I won't last too long on
mf
Broad - way.
Broad - way,
Broad - way.
They say there's al - ways
but look - in' at them
I'll catch a Grey-hound
mag - ic in the air.
just gives me the blues,
bus for home, they all say.

B♭
A♭/B♭
4fr
But when you're walk - in' down that street
'cause how ya gon - na make some time
But they're dead wrong, I know they are,
C
F
E♭/F
and you ain't had e - nough to eat, the glit - ter rubs right
when all you got is one thin dime, and one thin dime won't
'cause I can play this here gui - tar, and I won't quit till
1, 2
off and you're no - where on Broad - way.
e - ven shine your shoes on Broad - way.
3
I'm a star on Broad - way.

ONE FINE DAY

Words and Music by GERRY GOFFIN
and CAROLE KING

F
Dm11
3fr
Dm7
be.
your side.
be - fore.
One fine day
Bb
C7
To Coda
1
F
you're gon - na want me for your girl.
Dm
Bb
Csus
3fr
2
F
Bb
F
girl.

Cm7 F/G Cm7 F Cm F6
3fr
Though I know you're the
Cm7 F/G Cm7 F Cm7 F
kind of boy
B♭ B♭maj7
who on - ly wants to run a -
B♭6 B♭ (add9) Dm7 D7sus/A Dm7
6fr
round. I'll keep

G Dm7 G6 Dm7 D7sus/A Dm7 G F/G G
wait - ing, and some - day, dar - ling,
C B♭/C Gm7/C B♭/C C
D.S. al Coda
you'll come to me when you want to set - tle down, oh.
CODA
F Dm11 Dm7
3fr
girl. One fine day,
B♭ C F
oh, oh, one fine

Dm11
3fr
Dm7
B♭
C
day ___ you're gon - na want me for your
F
Dm7
girl. Shoo - be - do - be - do - be - do - be - do wah, wah,
(Lead vocal 1st time only)
B♭
Gm7/C
shoo - be - do - be - do - be - do - be - do wah, wah.
F
Dm7
B♭
B♭/C
Repeat and Fade
Instrumental ad lib. and fade

1 2 3

Words and Music by LEONARD BORISOFF,
JOHN MADARA and DAVID WHITE

C
Gm7/C
fall in love. It's
do it, too. It's
fight it, 'cause it's
eas - y, like tak - ing can -
C
To Coda
1
Gm7/C
2
Gm7/C
- dy from a ba - by.
- by.
C7
Ba - by, there's noth - in' hard a - bout love.
Bas - ic - 'ly it's as eas - y as pie.
The hard part is

D.S. al Coda
liv - in' with - out love. With - out your love, ba - by, I would die.
CODA
Gm7/C
C
- by.
eas - y. One, two, three,
Gm7
C7
F
oh, that's how el - e - men - t'ry it's gon - na be.
Fm
Repeat and Fade
Come on, let's fall in love. It's

(You've Got)
PERSONALITY

Words and Music by LLOYD PRINCE
and HAROLD LOGAN

C7
F
F♯dim7
o - ver, my friends say I'm a fool. But
o - ver, they still say I'm a fool. But
C
B♭7
A7
D9
4fr
G7
o - ver and o - ver, I'll be a fool for
o - ver and o - ver, I'll be a fool for
C
N.C.
G7
you.
you.
'Cause you've got per - son - al - i - ty, walk, a - per - son - al - i - ty, talk,
C
G7
a - per - son - al - i - ty, smile, a - per - son - al - i - ty, charm, a - per - son - al - i - ty, love

C F9 C7
a - per - son - al - i - ty, and 'course you've got a great big heart. So,
F F♯dim7 C B♭7♭5
o - ver and o - ver, oh, I'll be a fool for you.
A7 D7 G7
Now, o - ver and o - ver,
C F6 1 C G7♯5 2 C C6
what more can I do? do?

RAINDROPS

Words and Music by
DEE CLARK

Eb Cm Ab Fm7/Bb Eb Cm
3fr 3fr 4fr 3fr 3fr
left me ___ I'm so all a - lone, ___
Ab Fm7/Bb Eb Cm Ab G7
4fr 3fr 3fr 4fr
___ I would bring her back to me ___ but I don't know where she's
Cm Eb Eb7
3fr 3fr
gone, ___ I don't know where she's gone. There
Ab Gm Fm
4fr 3fr
must be a cloud in my head, ___ rain keeps fall - ing from my

E♭ G Cm F7
eye - eyes. Oh no, it can't be tear - drops 'cause a man ain't sup-posed to
B♭7 Fm7 B♭7 Fm7 B♭7 N.C. E♭ Cm A♭ Fm7/B♭
cry. So it must be rain - drops, so man-y
E♭ Cm A♭ Fm7/B♭ E♭ Cm A♭ G7
rain - drops, it feels like rain - drops fall-ing from my
Cm E♭
eye - eyes, fall-ing from my eyes.

PLEASE MR. POSTMAN

Words and Music by ROBERT BATEMAN,
GEORGIA DOBBINS, WILLIAM GARRETT,
FREDDIE GORMAN and BRIAN HOLLAND

E
such a long time for me to hear from that boy of mine?
A
F♯m
There must be some word to - day from my boy - friend
D
E
so far a - way. Please, Mis - ter Post - man, look and see if there's a let - ter, a
A
let - ter for me. I've been stand - ing here wait - ing, Mis - ter Post - man,

F♯m
D
so patient - ly, for just a card or just a let-ter,
E
A
say-ing he's re-turn-ing home to me. Mis-ter Post - man,
(Please, Mis - ter Post - man,
F♯m
oh yeah, please, please,
look and see if there's a let - ter in your bag for me.
D
E
Mis - ter Post - man, whoa yeah.
Why's it tak - ing such a long time for me to hear from that boy of mine?)

A
F♯m
Sax solo ad lib.
D
D/E
E
(Ah,
ah.)
Solo ends
A
F♯m
So man - y days you passed me by, see the tears stand - ing
D
in my eyes.
You did - n't stop to make me feel bet - ter,

E
A
by leav-ing me a card or a let - ter. Mis-ter Post - man,
(Please Mis - ter Post - man,
F♯m
oh yeah,
please, please, Mis - ter
look and see
if there's a let - ter in your bag for me.
D
E
Post - man. Why don't you check it and see one more
Why's it tak - ing such a long time?)
A
time for me? You got to wait a min - ute, wait a min - ute.

F♯m
D
Wait a min-ute, wait a min-ute. Ooh, Mis-ter Post -
(Mis-ter Post-man,
E
- man. Come on, de - liv-er the let - ter, the soon-er the bet - ter.
look and see.)
A
F♯m
(Vocal 1st time only)
Mis - ter Post - man.
D
E
Repeat ad lib. and Fade
Ah, ah.

POOR LITTLE FOOL

Words and Music by
SHARON SHEELEY

Easy Rock
C Am F G
mf
(Ooh.) I
C Am F
used to play a - round with hearts that has - tened at my
play a - round and tease me with her care - free dev - il
told me how she cared for me, that we'd nev - er
next day she was gone and I knew she lied to
played this game with oth - er hearts but I nev - er thought I'd
G C Am
call. But when I met that lit - tle girl I
eyes. She'd hold me close and kiss me, but her
part. And so for the ver - y first time I
me. She left me with a bro - ken heart,
see the day when some - one else would play love's

F
G7
C
Am
knew that I would fall,
heart was full of lies,
gave a - way my heart,
won her vic - to - ry,
fool - ish game with me,
poor lit - tle fool, oh yeah.
3
Dm7/F
G9
C
Am
I was a fool, uh - huh.
(Uh - huh, poor lit - tle fool.
3
F
To Coda
1-3
G
4
G
D.S. al Coda
I was a fool, oh yeah.)
She'd
She
The
yeah.)
Well, I've
CODA
G
C
yeah, oh yeah.)

ROMEO AND JULIET
(Just Like)

Words and Music by FREDDIE GORMAN
and BOB HAMILTON

C
F
G7
C
be writ-ten down in his-to-ry
be writ-ten down in his-to-ry
be de-stroyed by a trag-e-dy
just like Ro-me-o and Jul-i-et.
3rd time To Coda
F
Talk_ a-bout
C
D7
love and ro-mance, just wait till I get my-self straight. I'm a-gon-na put
G7
G7♯5
D.C. al Coda
CODA
Ro-me-o's fame right smack dab out-ta date.

SAVE THE LAST DANCE FOR ME

Words and Music by DOC POMUS
and MORT SHUMAN

Moderately, with a beat

B♭7 E♭7 A♭
Just don't for - get who's tak - ing you home and in whose arms you're
E♭ B♭7
gon - na be. So, dar - lin', save the
1 E♭ 2 E♭
last dance for me. Oh, I me.
N.C. B♭7
Ba - by, don't you know I love you so? Can't you feel it when we

E♭
3fr
N.C.
B♭7
touch? I will nev - er, nev - er let you go.
E♭
3fr
I love you, oh, so much. You can
dance, go and car - ry on till the night is gone till it's
B♭7
time to go. If he / she asks if you're

E♭
3fr
all a - lone, can {he / she} take you home, you've got to tell {him / her} no.
B♭7
E♭7
A♭
4fr
'Cause don't for - get who's tak - ing you home and in whose arms you're
E♭
3fr
B♭7
gon - na be. So, dar - lin', save the last dance for
1
E♭
3fr
me. You can
2
E♭
3fr
me.

SEA OF LOVE

Words and Music by GEORGE KHOURY
and PHILIP BAPTISTE

G
C
To Coda
1
G
love you.
love you.
2
G
D
C
Come with me
D
C
B7
to the sea of
D.C. al Coda
D
D7
love.
CODA
G
N.C.

Eb
Db
Come with me
Eb
Db
to the sea
C7
Eb
Eb7
Ab
of love. Come with me,
C7
Db
my love, to the sea, the

B♭7
A♭
sea of love.
I want to tell you
B♭7
A♭
D♭
just how much I love you.
A♭
I want to tell you,
B♭7
A♭
D♭
A♭
oh, how much I love you.
rit.

SHERRY

Words and Music by
BOB GAUDIO

Dm7 G7 C Am Dm7 G7
(Sher - ry, ba - by) Sher - ry, can you come out to -
(Sher - ry, ba - by) Tell her ev - 'ry - thing is all
1
C Am Dm7 G7
night? (Come, come, come out to - night.)
2
C E♭ 3fr F C N.C. E7
night? (Why don't you come on,) to my
right. (Why don't you come on,) put your
A7
Twist par - ty? (Come on,) where the
red dress on? (Come on,) mm, you

D7
bright moon shines. (Come on,) we'll dance the night a - way.
look so fine. (Come on,) move it nice and eas - y.
G7 N.C. G7 C Am
I'm gon - na make you mi - yi - yi - yine.
Girl, you make me lose my mind.
Sher -
Dm7 G7 C Am Dm7 G7
To Coda
- ry, ba - by, (Sher - ry, ba - by)
C Am Dm7 G7 C Am
Sher - ry, can you come out to - night? (Come, come,

Dm7 G7 C Am Dm7 G7
D.S. al Coda (no repeat)
come out to - night, come, come, come out to - night.)
CODA
C Am Dm7 G7
Sher - ry, can you come out to -
C Am Dm7 G7
night? (Come, come, come out to - night.)
C Am Dm7 G7
Repeat and Fade
Come, come, come out to - night.
Sher - ry, Sher - ry, ba - by.

THE SHOOP SHOOP SONG
(It's in His Kiss)

Words and Music by
RUDY CLARK

A F♯m Bm7 E7 A D
wan - na know if he loves you so, it's in his kiss.
wan - na know if he loves you so, it's in his kiss.
(That's where it is.)
1 E7 F♯7
(Is it
2 A
End instrumental
C♯7
Kiss him, (hug him) and
F♯m7
squeeze him tight, and find out what you wan - na know.

B7
E7
If it's love, if it real - ly is, it's there in his
F♯7
Bm7
E7
Bm7
E7
kiss. (How 'bout the way he acts?) Oh, no, that's not the way, and
Bm7
E7
Bm7
E7
A
F♯m
you're not lis - t'nin' to all that I say. If you wan - na know if he

To Coda
Bm7
E7
A
D
loves you so, it's in his kiss.
E
F♯7
D.S. al Coda
Instrumental
CODA
Repeat and Fade
A
D
E7
kiss. (That's where it is.)
Optional Ending
A
D
A
It's in his kiss. (That's where it is.)

SILHOUETTES

Words and Music by FRANK C. SLAY JR.
and BOB CREWE

Slow beat tempo
F
Dm
Gm7
C7
mf
F
Dm
Gm7
C7
F
Dm
Gm
C7
F
Dm
Took a walk and passed your house late last night, all the shades were pulled and
Gm
C7
F
Dm
Gm
C7
drawn 'way down tight, from with-in a dim light cast two sil-hou-ettes on the

F Dm Gm C7 F Dm
shade, oh what a love - ly cou - ple they made.
Put his her arms a - round your
Gm C7 F Dm Gm C7
waist, held you tight, kiss - es I could al - most taste in the
F Dm Gm C7 F Dm
night, won - dered why I'm not the guy girl whose sil - hou - ette's on the shade, I could - n't hide the
Gm C7 F C7 F Dm Gm C7
tears in my eyes.
Ah,
3fr

F D7 Gm C7 F D7 G Em
3fr
Lost con-trol, and rang your
Am D7 G Em Am D7
bell, I was sore, "Let me in, or else I'll beat down your
G Em Am D7 G Em
3
3
door," when two stran - gers, who had been two sil - hou - ettes on the shade, said to my shock, "You're
Am D7 G Em Am D7
on the wrong block." Rushed down to your house with wings on my

G Em Am D7 G Em
feet, loved you like I've nev - er loved you, my sweet, vowed that you and I would
Am D7 G Em Am D7 G D7
3 3 3 3
be two sil - hou-ettes on the shade all of our days, two sil - hou-ettes on the shade.
G Em Am D7
Ah.
G E7
1 Am D7
2 Am D7 G

SINCE I MET YOU BABY

Words and Music by
IVORY JOE HUNTER

Slow Blues
C G7 C
mp
8va
G7 C F C Dm
Since I met you, ba - by, my whole life has changed.
Since I met you, ba - by, I'm a hap - py man.
C C7 F
Since I met you, ba - by, my whole life has changed.
Since I met you, ba - by, I'm a hap - py man.
C G7
To Coda
And ev-'ry-bod-y tells me that I am not the
I'm gon-na try to please you in ev-'ry way I

C G7 C F C Dm
same. I don't need no-bod-y to tell my trou-bles to,
8va
C C7 F
I don't need no-bod-y to tell my trou-bles to,
8va
C G7
'cause since I met you, ba-by, all I need is
8va
C G7
D.S. al Coda
you.
8va
CODA
C G7 C
can.

SINCERELY

Words and Music by ALAN FREED
and HARVEY FUQUA

Slowly, with a good beat
F6 Dm7 Gm7 C7 F6 Dm7
mf
Gm7 C7 C9♯5 F6 Dm7 Gm7 C7 F6 Dm7
Sin - cere - ly, oh! Yes, sin - cere - ly,
Gm7 C7 F6 Dm7 Gm7 C7
'cause I love you so dear - ly, please say you'll be
F6 Dm7 Gm7 C7 C9♯5 F6 Dm7
mine. Sin - cere - ly,

Gm7 C7 F6 Dm7 Gm7 C7
oh, you know how I love you, I'll do an - y - thing
F6 Dm7 Gm7 C7 F6 Gm7
for you, please say you'll be mine.
G♯dim F7 B♭6 B♭m6
Oh, Lord, won't you tell me why I
F6 Fmaj7 F9 G7 Dm7
love that {fel - la / girl - ie} so? {He / She} does - n't

Gm7 C9 C9♯5
want me, oh, I'll never - er, nev - er, nev - er, nev - er let (him / her) go. Sin -
F6 Dm7 Gm7 C7 F6 Dm7
cere - ly, oh, you know how I love you,
Gm7 C7 F6 Dm7 Gm7 C7
I'll do an - y - thing for you, please say you'll be
1 F6 Dm7 Gm7 C7 C9♯5
mine. Sin -
2 F6 Dm7 Gm7 G♭6/9 F6/9
mine.
8fr

SIXTEEN CANDLES

Words and Music by LUTHER DIXON
and ALLYSON R. KHENT

Eb Ebmaj7 Eb7 Ab
can - dles, make your wish come true, for I'll be
Bb7 Fm7 Bb7 Eb Ab
wish - ing that you love me, too.
Eb9 Eb7 Ab A6 Ab Bb7
You're on - ly six - teen, but you're my teen - age
Eb6 Bbm C7
queen. You're the pret - ti - est, love - li - est
3fr
4fr

B♭m C7 Fm7 B♭7
girl I've ev - er seen. Six - teen
E♭ E♭maj7 E♭7 A♭
can - dles in my heart will glow
B♭7 Fm7 B♭7
for ev - er and ev - er, for I love you
1 E♭ A♭ E♭ B♭7
so. Six - teen
2 E♭ A♭ E♭
so.
3fr
4fr
3

SLEEPWALK

By SANTO FARINA,
JOHN FARINA and ANN FARINA

C F C C7 F
Fm C C7
F Fm G7 A♭7
G7 A♭7 G7 C Am Fm G7
C Am Fm G7 C Am Fm G7
C Am A♭7 G7
C F7 C
rall.

STAGGER LEE

Words and Music by LLOYD PRICE
and HAROLD LOGAN

Freely
B♭ Gm Cm F7
The night was clear and the moon was yel - low, and the leaves came tum - bling
mp
Moderate Shuffle
B♭6 F7♯5 B♭ F7♯5 B♭7
down. I was stand - ing on the cor - ner when I
Lee told Bil - ly, "I can't
Lee went to the bar - room, and he
E♭7 B♭
heard my bull - dog bark. He was bark - ing at the two men who were
let you go with that. You have won all my mon - ey and my
stood a - cross the bar - room door. Said, "Now no - bod - y move," and he

F7 Bb6 F7 F7#5
gam - bling in the dark. It was
brand - new Stet - son hat." Stag - ger
pulled his for - ty - four. "Stag - ger
Bb F7 Bb7 Eb7
Stag - ger Lee and Bil - ly, two men who gam - ble
Lee went home, and he got his for - ty -
Lee," cried Bil - ly, "oh please, don't take my
Bb F7
late. Stag - ger Lee threw sev - en, Bil - ly swore that he threw
four. Said, "I'm go - ing to the bar - room just to pay that debt I
life. I got three lit - tle chil - dren and a ver - y sick - ly
1, 2 Bb6 F7 F7#5
eight. Stag - ger
owe." Stag - ger
3 Bb6 F7 F7#5
wife." Stag - ger

B♭ F7♯5 B♭7 E♭7
Lee shot Bil - ly. Oh, he shot that poor boy so bad, 'til the
B♭ F7 B♭ F7
bul - let came through Bil - ly, and it broke the bar - ten - der's glass. Look out now.
B♭ B♭7 E♭7
Go, Stag - ger Lee. Go, Stag - ger Lee. Go, Stag - ger Lee. Go, Stag - ger Lee.
B♭ F7 B♭6
Go, Stag - ger Lee. Go, Stag - ger Lee. Go, Stag - ger Lee. Go.

STAND BY ME

Words and Music by JERRY LEIBER,
MIKE STOLLER and BEN E. KING

F
see,
sea,
oh I won't be a - fraid,
I won't cry, I won't cry,
Dm
C
Dm
no I won't be a - fraid
no I won't shed a tear
just as
B♭
C
F
long as you stand, stand by me.
So dar - ling, dar - ling,
F
Dm
C
Dm
stand by me,
stand by me,
oh

B♭
C
F
stand,
stand by me,
stand by me.
1
2
F
If the
Dar-ling,
stand
by me,
Dm
C
Dm
B♭
stand by
me,
oh
stand,
C
F
Repeat and Fade
stand by me,
stand by me.
When-ev-er I'm in trou-ble, won't you

STAY

Words and Music by
MAURICE WILLIAMS

Moderately
B♭ Gm E♭ F7 B♭ Gm E♭ F7
mf
Dance just a lit-tle bit long-er.
Please, please, please, please tell me that you're go-in' to. Now, your
dad-dy don't mind and your mom-my don't mind.

E♭ F7 B♭ Gm E♭ F7
Could we have an - oth - er dance, dear, just a - one more,
Gm N.C. B♭ Gm
one more time? Oh, won't you stay
E♭ F7 B♭ Gm E♭ F7
just a lit - tle bit long - er? Please let me
B♭ Gm E♭ F7 B♭
dance. Please say that you will.
3fr
3

SURF CITY

Words and Music by BRIAN WILSON
and JAN BERRY

Fm
Ab
old - ie, but a good - ie.
got a par - ty go - in'.
ride in my wet suit.
Surf Cit - y, here we come!
Well, it
There's
When I
Db
Bbm
Gb
ain't got a back - seat or a rear win - dow,
but it still gets me where I
two swing - in' hon - eys for ev - 'ry guy
and all you got - ta do is just
get to Surf Cit - y I'll be shoot - in' the curl
and pick - in' out the par - ties for the
Eb
Eb7
Ab
wan - na go.
wink your eye.
surf - er girl.
And I'm goin' to Surf Cit - y 'cause it's
two to one. You know I'm goin' to Surf Cit - y, gon - na have some fun. Yeah, I'm

D♭
A♭
4fr
goin' to Surf Cit - y 'cause it's two to one. You know I'm goin' to Surf Cit - y, gon - na
E
F♯7
have some fun. Two girls for ev - 'ry
1, 2
E♭
3fr
3
C
boy!
They say they
And if my
two girls for
F
G7
C
ev - 'ry boy!

TAKE GOOD CARE OF MY BABY

Words and Music by GERRY GOFFIN
and CAROLE KING

Dm/F
Gm7
C9
F
F7
ev - er make her blue.
Just tell her that you love her,
ev - er make her cry.
Just let your love sur - round her,
B♭
B♭m
F/C
1
Dm
Gm7
make sure you're think - in' of her in ev - 'ry - thing you say and do.
paint a rain - bow all a - round her. Don't let her
C9
2
Gm7
C7
F
Gm7
see a cloud - y sky.
Once up - on a
C7
F
Dm7
Gm7
C7
time that lit - tle girl was mine.
If I had been true, I

Fmaj7 Dm7 Gm7 C7 F Dm/F Gm7
know she'd nev - er be with you. So, take good care of my ba -
C7 F Dm/F Gm7 C9
by, be just as kind as you can be,
F F7 B♭ B♭m F/C
and if you should dis - cov - er that you don't real - ly love her, just send my
Dm Gm7 C7 F
ba - by back home to me.

TEARS ON MY PILLOW

Words and Music by SYLVESTER BRADFORD
and AL LEWIS

Moderately, in 4
C Am Dm G7 C Am Dm G7
mf
C Am Dm G7
You don't re - mem - ber me, but I re - mem - ber you.
C Am Dm G7
'Twas not so long a - go you broke my heart in two.

F G7 F G7
Tears on my pil - low, pain in my heart caused by
C Am Dm G7 C Am
you. If we could start a - new,
Dm G7 C Am
I would - n't hes - i - tate. I'd glad - ly take you back
Dm G7 F G7
and tempt the hand of fate. Tears on my pil - low,

F G7 C F G7 C F C
pain in my heart caused by you. Hoo hoo hoo hoo hoo.
F G7 C F G7 C
Love is not a gadget, love is not a toy.
F♯7 G7 F♯7 G7
When you find the one you love {she'll / he'll} fill your heart with joy.
C Am Dm G7
Before you go away, my darling, think of me.

C Am Dm G7
There may be still a chance to end my mis - er - y.
F G7 F G7
Tears on my pil - low, pain in my heart caused by
1
C F C G7
you.
2
C F G7 C F C
you. Hoo hoo hoo hoo hoo.
rit.

TEEN ANGEL

Words and Music by
JEAN SURREY

D7
G
Teen an - gel, can you hear me? Teen an - gel, can you see — me?
C
D7
Are you some - where up a - bove and am I still your
1, 2
G
D7
G
own — true love?
What
Just
3
G
own — true love?
Freely
Em
C
D7
G
Teen an - gel, teen an - gel, an - swer me, please.
rit.

A TEENAGER IN LOVE

Words and Music by DOC POMUS
and MORT SHUMAN

Moderately slow
C
Am
F
G7
mp
Each time we have a quar - rel it al - most breaks my heart,
One day I feel so hap - py; next day I feel so sad.
'cause I am so a - fraid that we will have to part.
I guess I'll learn to take the good with the bad.
Each night I ask the stars up a - bove:

C
N.C.
G7
Why must I be a teen - ag - er in love?
F
G7
F
G7
I cried a tear for no - bod - y but you.
F
G7
F
G7
I'll be a lone - ly one if you should say we're through.
C
Am
F
G7
If you want to make me cry, that won't be so hard to do.

C
Am
F
G7
And if you should say good - bye, I'll still go on lov - ing you.
C
Am
F
G7
Each night I ask the stars up a - bove:
C
N.C.
G7
Why must I be a teen - ag - er in love, in
1
C
F7
G7
love?
2
C
F7
C
love?

TELL LAURA I LOVE HER

Words and Music by JEFF BARRY
and BEN RALEIGH

B♭
E♭
Dm
a thou-sand dol-lar prize, it read. He could-n't get Lau-ra
E♭
F
on the phone, so to her moth-er Tom-my said:
B♭
"Tell Lau-ra I love her! Tell Lau-ra I
Cm
B♭
E♭6
need her! Tell Lau-ra I may be late, I've some-thing to do

F7
B♭
that can - not wait."
E♭
3fr
B♭
He drove his car to the rac - ing grounds;
he was the young-est
E♭
3fr
Dm
E♭
3fr
driv - er there.
The crowd roared as they start - ed the race; 'round the
3
F
B♭
track they drove at a dead - ly pace!
No one knows what

E♭
B♭
E♭
3fr
hap-pened that day, how his car o-ver-turned in flames, but
Dm
E♭
F
as they pulled him from the twist-ed wreck, with his dy-ing breath, they
B♭
3
heard him say: "Tell Lau-ra I love her!
Cm
B♭
Tell Lau-ra I need her! Tell Lau-ra not to cry, my

E♭6
F7
B♭
To Coda
love for her will nev - er die!”
E♭
B♭
Now, in the chap - el Lau - ra prays
for her Tom - my who
E♭
Dm
E♭
passed a - way. It was just for Lau - ra he lived and died; a -
F
D.S. al Coda
lone in the chap - el she can hear him cry:
CODA

THERE GOES MY BABY

Words and Music by JERRY LEIBER,
MIKE STOLLER, BEN E. NELSON,
LOVER PATTERSON and GEORGE TREADWELL

Am
heart ___ and made her cry. ___
Dm7
G7
Now I'm a - lone, ___ so all a - lone. ___ What can I do?
Dm7
G7
C
What can I do? ___ There goes my ba - by. ___
Am
Dm7
There goes my ba - by. ___ There goes my

G7
Dm7
G7
ba - by. There she goes. Yes, I wan - na know did she
C
Am
love me? Did she real - ly love me?
left me. Why did she leave me
3
3
Dm7
3
Was she just play - ing me for a
so all a - lone, so all a -
3
3
3
1
G7
fool? I won - der why she
3
2
G7
Dm7
lone? I
3

G7
C
was gon - na tell her that I love her
Am
and that I need her
be - side my
Dm7
G7
side
to be my guide.
I wan - na
Dm7
G7
C
know,
where is my,
where is my

Am
Dm7
ba - by?
I want my ba - by,
G7
Dm7
C
I need my ba - by,
yes.
Oh,
Am
oh,
G7
C
C6
oh.

WAH WATUSI

Words and Music by KAL MANN
and DAVE APPELL

G Em G Em G Em
(1.) Wah wah wa - tu - si,
(2.) wah wah wa - tu - si,
(3., 4.) wah wah wa - tu - si,
G Em C
oh, ba - by, it's the dance
c' - mon and take a chance
oh, ba - by, it's the dance
Am7 D7 G Em G Em
made a - for ro - mance.
and get a - with this dance.
made a - for ro - mance.

C
Am7
C7
G
Em
Ba - by, ba - by, when y' do the twist, never, never do you
Ba - by, ba - by, when you do the fly, your arms are wast - in' wav - in'
Ba - by, ba - by, that's the way it goes, noth - in' hap - pens when you
G
C
Am7
get your - self kissed, 'cause you're al - ways danc - in'
in the sky, c' - mon and hold me like a
mashed po - ta - toes, I just got - ta fall in
C7
D7
3rd time Repeat and Fade
far a - part, wa - tu - si girl is a - real - ly smart. Wah
lov - er should, wa - tu - si makes you feel so good. Wah
love with you, wa - tu - si is the dance to do. Wah

THE TWIST

Words and Music by
HANK BALLARD

C7
G
G7
and go like this.
tear the house down.
and she knows how to twist.
Ee oh,
Ee oh, twist,
Ee oh,
C7
ba - by, ba - by, twist ('round and a - round and a - round and a-) just,
G
D7
just like this. ('Round and a - round.) Come on, lit - tle miss,
C7
G
1, 2
3
and do the twist. ('Round and a - round.)
While Dad - dy is
You should
round.)

WHERE THE BOYS ARE

Words and Music by HOWARD GREENFIELD
and NEIL SEDAKA

Dm Cm7 F7 B♭
boys are, my true love will be. He's
Cm7 F7 B♭ Gm Cm7 F7
walk - ing down some street in town and I know he's look - ing there for
B♭ Cm7 F7 B♭
me. In the crowd of a mil - lion peo - ple, I'll
F7 B♭ Cm7 F7
find my Val - en - tine, Then I'll climb to the

B♭
C7
high - est stee - ple and tell the world he's mine.
B♭
Gm
Dm
Cm7
F7
Till he holds me I wait im - pa - tient -
Dm7♭5
G7
Cm
Dm7
ly. Where the boys are, where the boys are, where the
Cm7
F7
1 B♭
F7
2 B♭
boys are, some - one waits for me. me.
rit.

WHY DO FOOLS FALL IN LOVE

Words and Music by MORRIS LEVY
and FRANKIE LYMON

F Dm7 Gm7 C7 F Dm7 Gm7 C7 F Dm7
break of day? Why do they fall in love? Why
Gm7 C7 F Dm7 Gm7 C7 F Dm7
does the rain fall from up a - bove? Why do fools fall in love?
Gm7 C7 F B♭6 B♭m6
Why do they fall in love?
Love is a los - ing game,
Why does my heart
F F7 B♭6 B♭m6
love can be a shame. I know of a fool, you see,
skip a cra - zy beat? For I know

G7 C7 F Dm7 Gm7 C7
for that fool is me! Tell me why,
it will reach de - feat!
F Dm7 Gm7 C7 F Dm7 Gm7 C7 F Dm7
tell me why!
1 Gm7 C7 2 F F7 B♭ C7
Why do fools
F Dm7 Gm7 C7 F
fall in love?

WILD ONE

Words and Music by KAL MANN,
BERNIE LOWE and DAVE APPELL

A7
D7
You lit - tle doll, all you do is play.
You've got the look that I'm mad a - bout.
You got a new ba - by
I've got the lips that - 'll
1
ev - 'ry day, but some - day
it's gon - na be
G
N.C.
G
N.C.
G
me, me, and on - ly me, ah.
2
knock you out. Come on,
C
F
G
C
G
D.S. al Coda
wild one; be wild a - bout me, oh, yeah.

CODA
E7/B C B B♭ A7
Solo ends (Wah, wah, wah.) You lit - tle doll, all you do is play.
D7
You got a new ba - by ev - 'ry day, but some - day
G N.C. G N.C. A♭
it's gon - na be me, me, and on - ly me. Oh,
D♭ A♭
wild one, I'll make you set - tle down,
4fr

A♭7
4fr
(set - tle down,) uh huh. Wild one, I'm gon - na clip your
D♭
F7/C
3fr
B♭7
wings, (yeah, yeah,) and then sing, (yeah, yeah.) You've got the lips that I'm
E♭7
mad a - bout, ah. I got the lips that - 'll knock you out. Come on,
D♭
G♭
A♭
4fr
D♭
wild one; be wild a - bout me, oh,

C
Cb
Bb7
yeah, (wah, wah, wah.)
Instrumental solo
Eb7
Db
Gb
Solo ends
Come on, wild one;
Ab
4fr
N.C.
be wild about me.
1
Db
C
Cb
me. One more one! (Wah, wah, wah.)
2
Db
Gb
Ab
4fr
Db
me, be wild about me.

WONDERFUL! WONDERFUL!

Words by BEN RALEIGH
Music by SHERMAN EDWARDS

Smoothly
mf
Bb6 Eb6 Bb6 Eb6 Bb6 Eb6 Bb6 Eb6
Bb6 Eb6 Bb6 Eb6 Bb6 Eb6
Some - times we walk hand in hand by the sea and we breathe in the cool salt - y
Some - times we stand on the top of a hill and we gaze at the earth and the
Bb6 Eb6 Ab6 Eb6 Ab6
air; you turn to me with a kiss in your eyes and my
sky; I turn to you and you melt in my arms, there we
Eb Cm7 Cm6 D7 Gm G7
heart feels a thrill be - yond com - pare! Then your lips cling to mine, it's
are, dar - ling, on - ly you and I! What a mo - ment to share, it's

Cm7 3fr
E♭m6
1
B♭
C9
F7
wonderful! wonderful! Oh, so wonderful, my love!
wonderful! wonderful!
2
B♭
Cm7 3fr
F7
B♭
E♭maj7 3fr
E♭6
Fm7
B♭7
Oh, so wonderful, my love! This world is full of wondrous things, it's
E♭ 3fr
Gm7
E♭6
C7
F7
true, but they wouldn't have much meaning without you.
B♭6
E♭6
B♭6
E♭6
B♭6
E♭6
Some quiet evenings I sit by your side and we're lost in a world of our

B♭6 E♭6 A♭6 E♭6 A♭6
own; I feel the glow of your un - spo - ken love, I'm a -
E♭ Cm7 Cm6 D7 Gm G7
ware of the treas - ure that I own. And I say to my - self, it's
Cm7 E♭m6 B♭ Cm7 F7 B♭6 E♭6
won - der - ful! won - der - ful! Oh, so won - der - ful, my love!
B♭6 E♭6 B♭

WILL YOU LOVE ME TOMORROW
(Will You Still Love Me Tomorrow)

Words and Music by GERRY GOFFIN
and CAROLE KING

Light Rock
Eb(add9) Eb Eb(add9) Eb Ab Abmaj7
mp
With pedal
Bb7sus Bb7 Eb(add9) Eb Bb/C Cm
Ab6 Abmaj7 Bb (add2) Eb(add9) Eb
To - night you're mine com - plete - ly.
Is this a last - ing treas - ure,
I'd like to know if your love
Eb(add9) Eb Ab Bb

Eb(add9) Eb Bb/C Cm Fm7/Bb
3fr
You give your love so sweet - ly.
or just a mo - ment's pleas - ure?
is love I can be sure of.
Bb7 Gsus G7
To - night, the light of love
Can I be - lieve the mag -
So tell me now and I
Cm Bb Cm/Bb Ab(add9)
4fr
is in your eyes. But will you
- ic of your sigh? Will you still
won't ask a - gain. Will you still
Bbsus Bb Eb(add9) Eb
To Coda
1
Bb/C Cm
love me to - mor - row, to -
love me to - mor - row?
love me to - mor - row,

2
A♭maj7
A♭6
3fr
B♭sus
B♭
mor - row?
cresc.
A♭
4fr
Gm
3fr
To - night with words un - spo - ken
mf
A♭
4fr
A♭/B♭
4fr
you say that I'm the on - ly one.
E♭
3fr
B♭/E♭
E♭
3fr
B♭/E♭
E♭
3fr
B♭/E♭
A♭
4fr
But will my

Gm
heart be bro - ken
when the night
Cm7 Fsus F7 Fm7 Gm7 A♭ Fm7/B♭
D.S. al Coda
meets the morn - ing sun?
dim.
CODA
B♭/C Cm E♭(add9) E♭ B♭/C Cm B♭/C
to - mor - row?
A♭ B♭ A♭ E♭
Will you still love me to - mor - row?
rit.

YOU'VE LOST THAT LOVIN' FEELIN'

Words and Music by BARRY MANN,
CYNTHIA WEIL and PHIL SPECTOR

Slowly
B♭/C
mf
You nev - er
B♭/C
C
close your eyes __ an - y - more when I kiss your lips. __
wel - come look __ in your eyes when I reach for you. __
B♭/C
__ And there's no ten - der - ness __ like be - fore in your fin - ger - tips. __
__ And, girl, you're start - ing to __ crit - i - cize lit - tle things __ I do. __

C
Dm7
You're try - ing hard not to show it,
It makes me just feel like cry - ing,
Em7
Fmaj7
F/G
G
but, ba - by, ba - by, I know it.
'cause, ba - by, some - thing beau - ti - ful's dy - ing.
(Ba - by)
C
Dm/C
G7
You've lost that lov - in' feel - in', whoa oh, that lov -
C
Dm/C
- in' feel - in'. You've lost that lov - in' feel - in'! Now it's

B♭/C
1
C
gone, gone, gone, whoa oh oh oh.
2
C F G F G
Now, there's no
C F G F G C F
Ba - by, ba - by, I'd get down on my knees for you.
G F G C F G F G
If that would make you love me like you used to

C F G F G
do.
C F G F G
We had a love, a love, a love you don't find ev - 'ry
C F G F G C F
day.
So don't, don't,
G F G C F G F G
don't, don't let it slip a - way.
3

C F G F G
Ba - by, ba - by, I beg you
(Ba - by,) (ba - by,)
C F G F G
please, please, I need your
(beg you please,) (please,)
C F G F G
love, I need your love, so bring it on
(I need your love,) (I need your love,)
C F G
back, so bring it on back.
(bring it on back,) (Bring it on back.)

C
Dm/C
G7
Bring back_ that lov - in' feel - in', whoa oh, that lov -
C
Dm/C
- in' feel - in'. Bring back that lov - in' feel - in', 'cause it's
B♭/C
gone, gone, gone, and I can't go
C
Repeat and Fade
on, whoa oh oh oh.